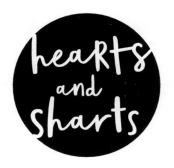

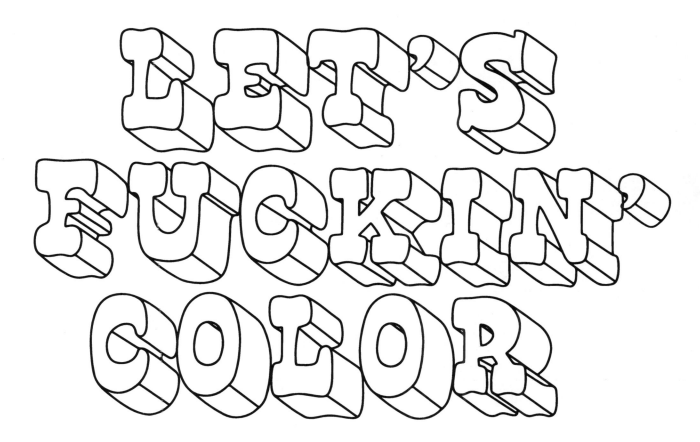

@HEARTSANDSHARTS

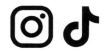

WWW.HEARTSANDSHARTS.COM
© 2024 HEARTS AND SHARTS

ISBN: 979-8-9904495-0-3

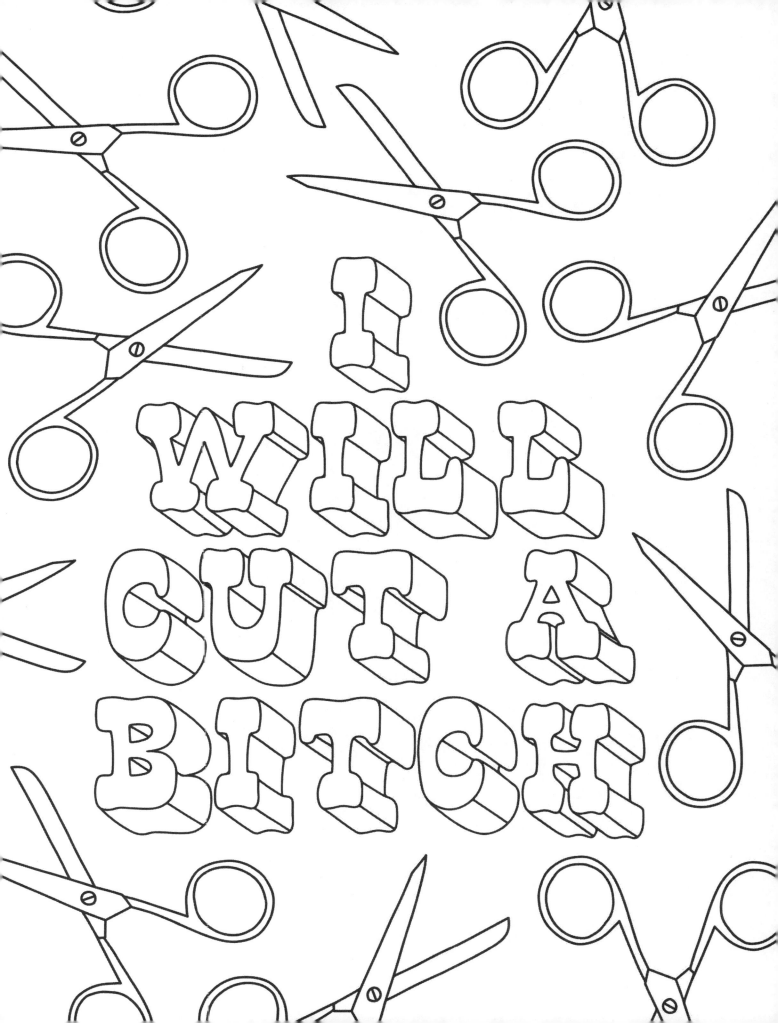

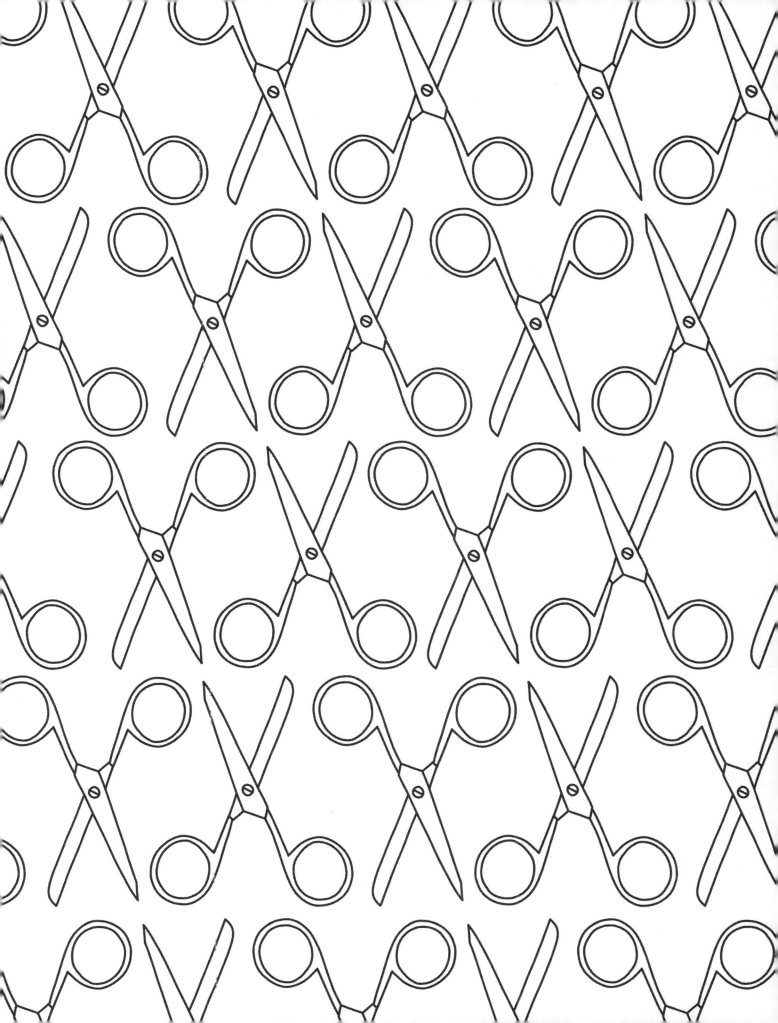

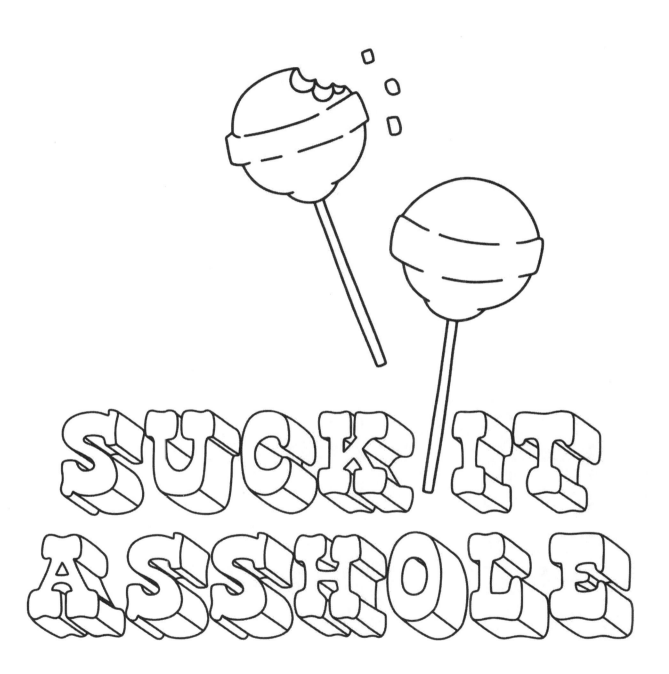

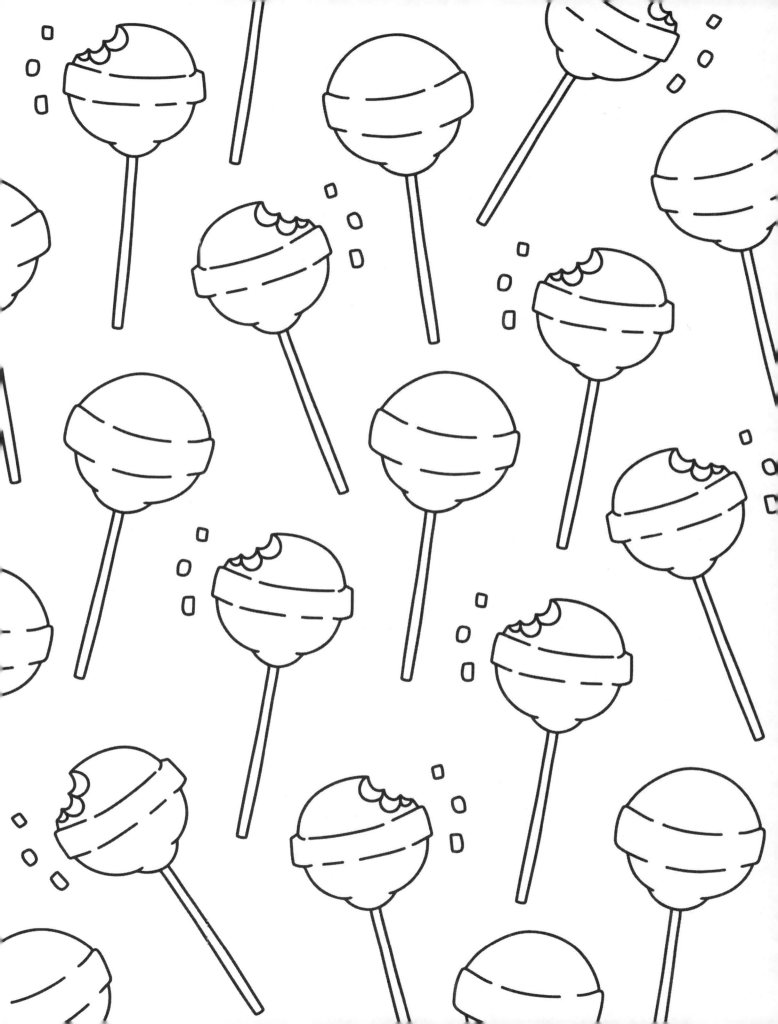

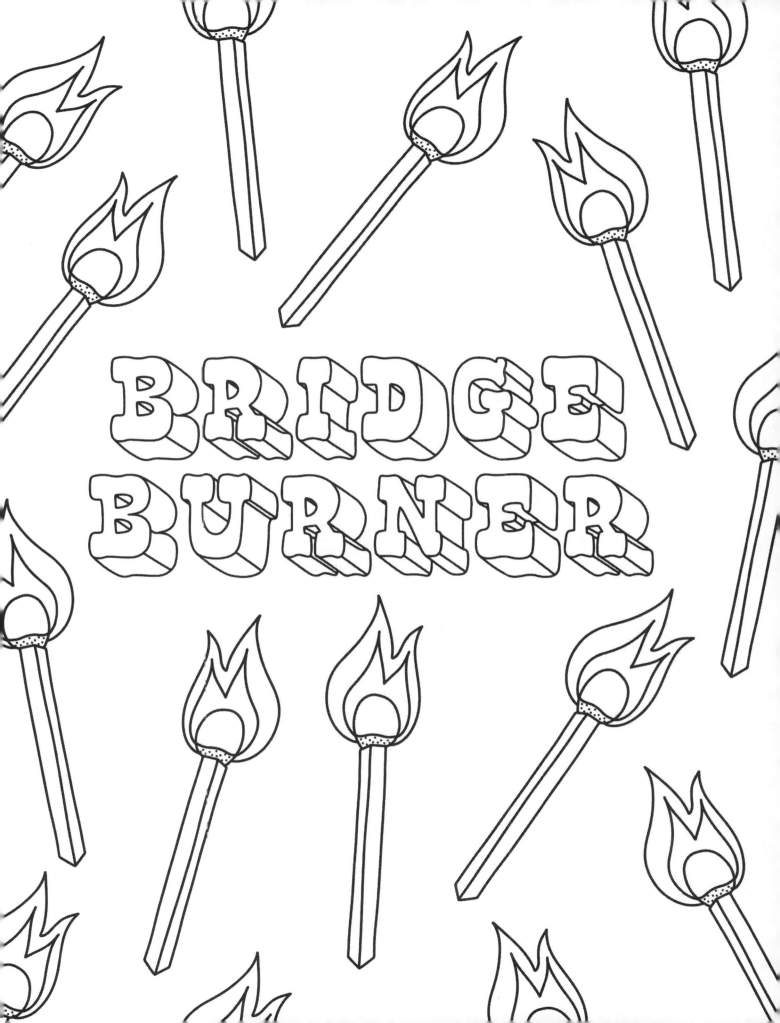

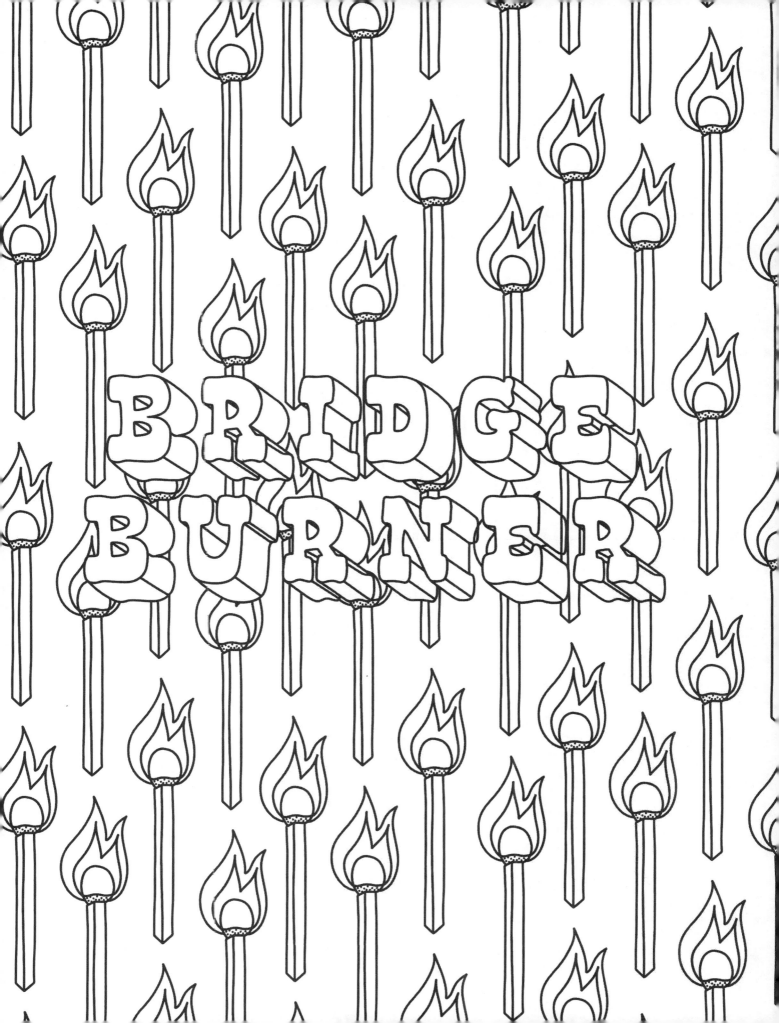

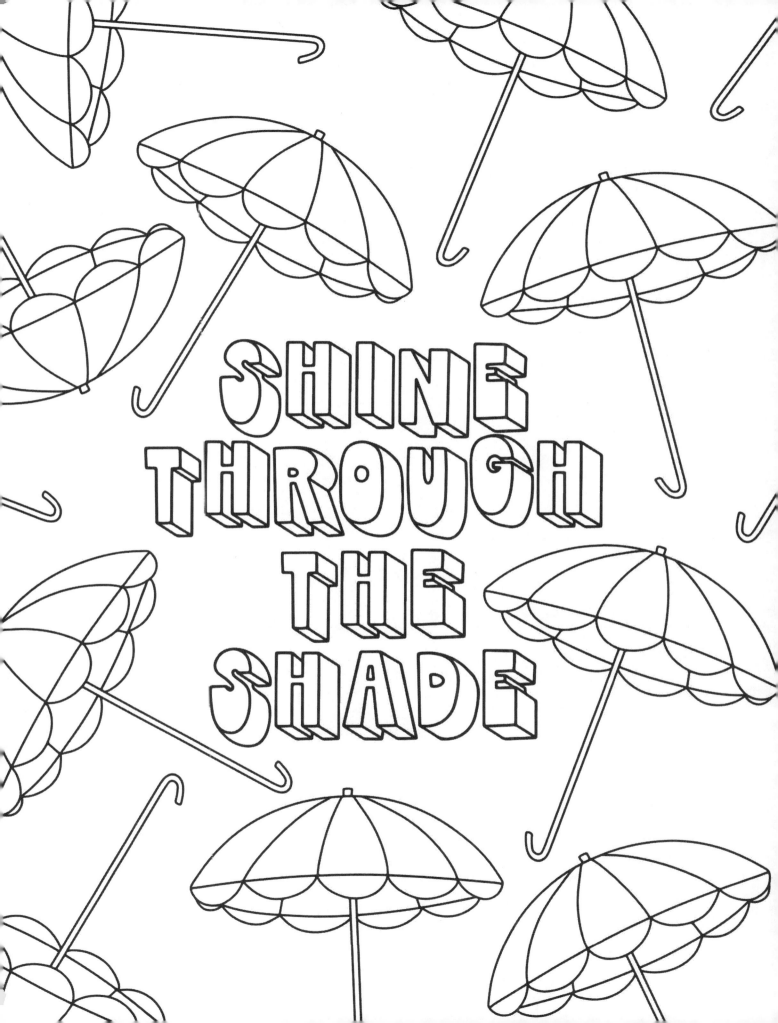

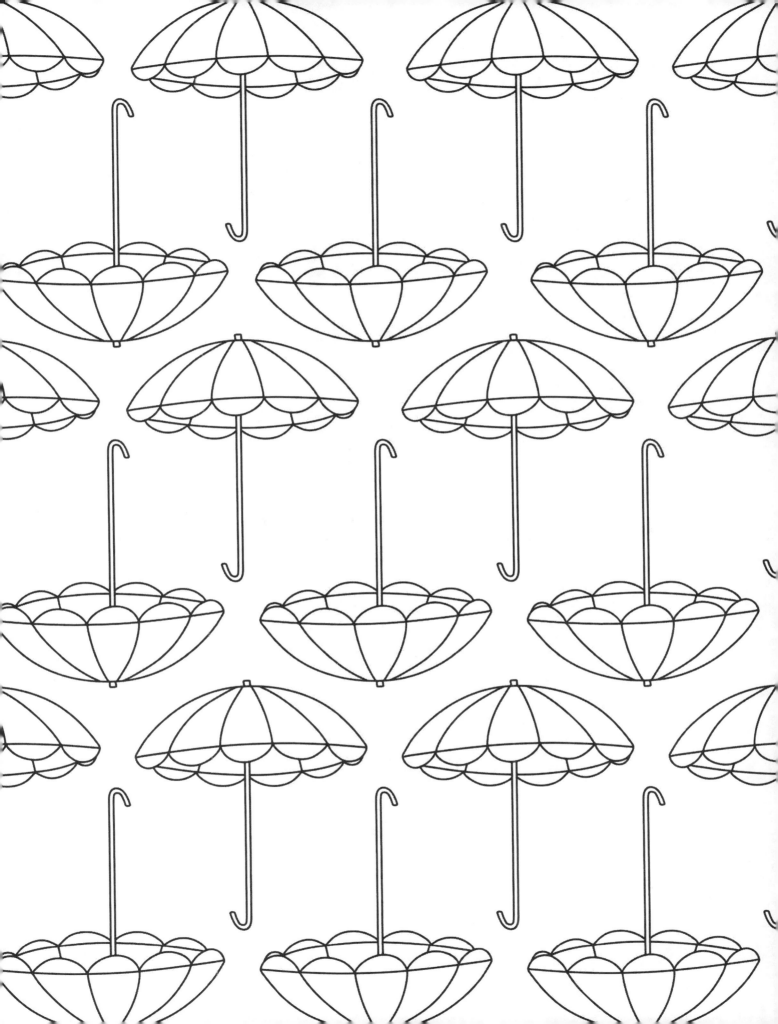

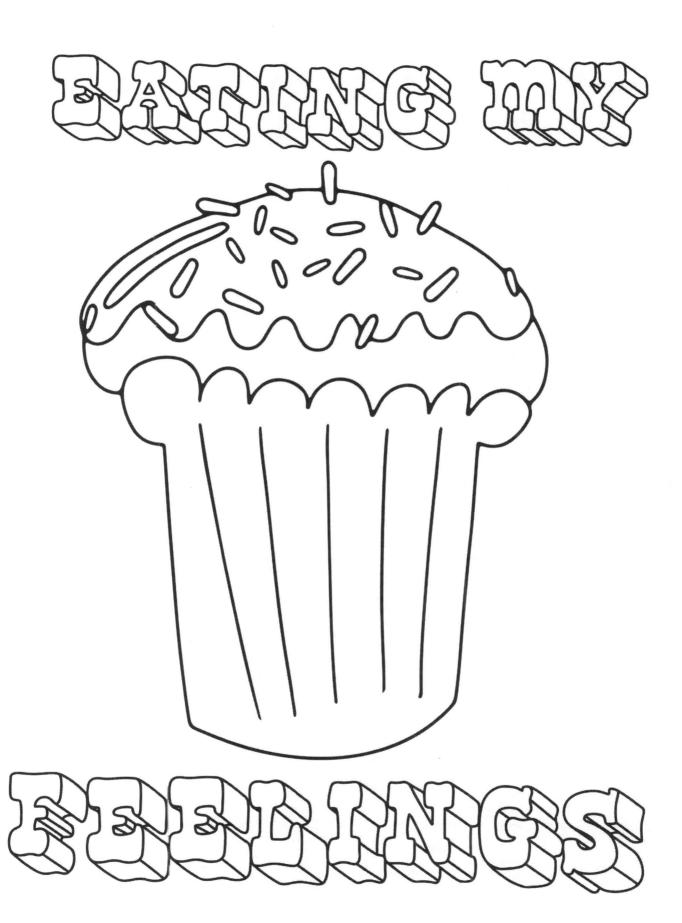

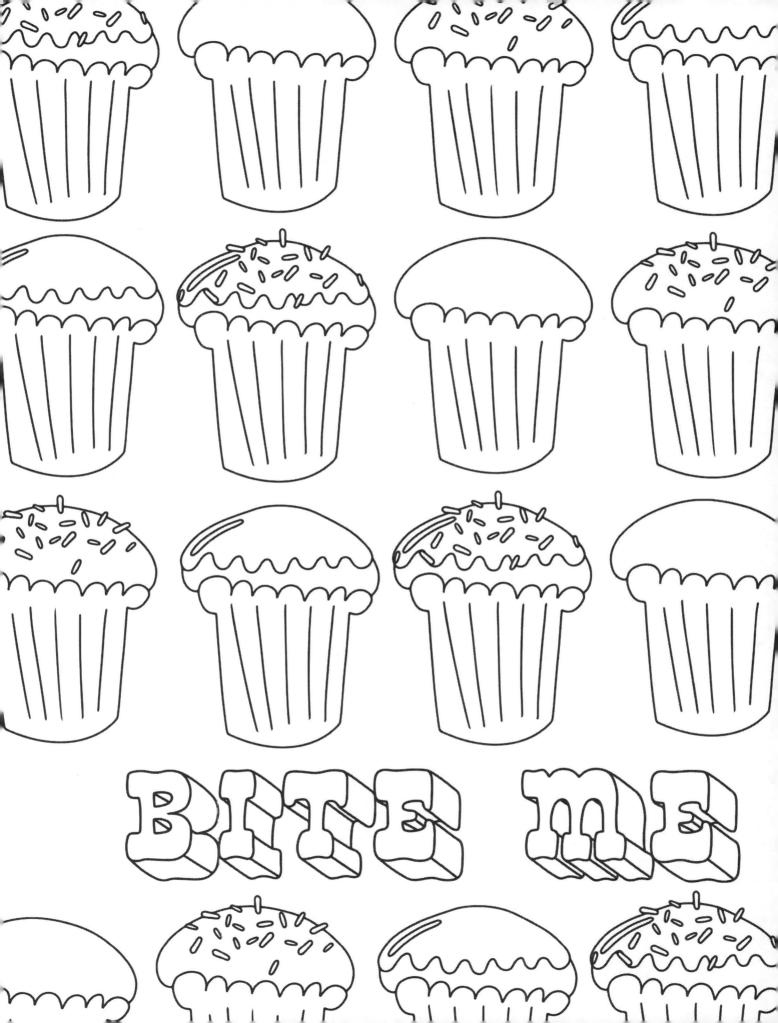

BETTER NOT BITTER

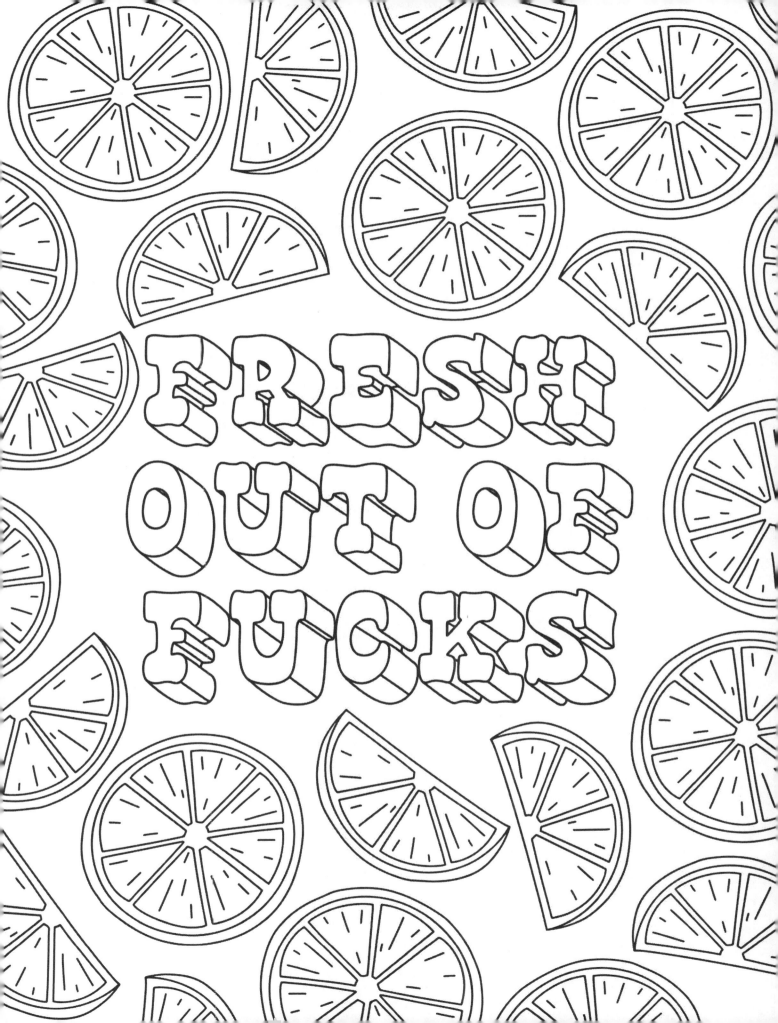

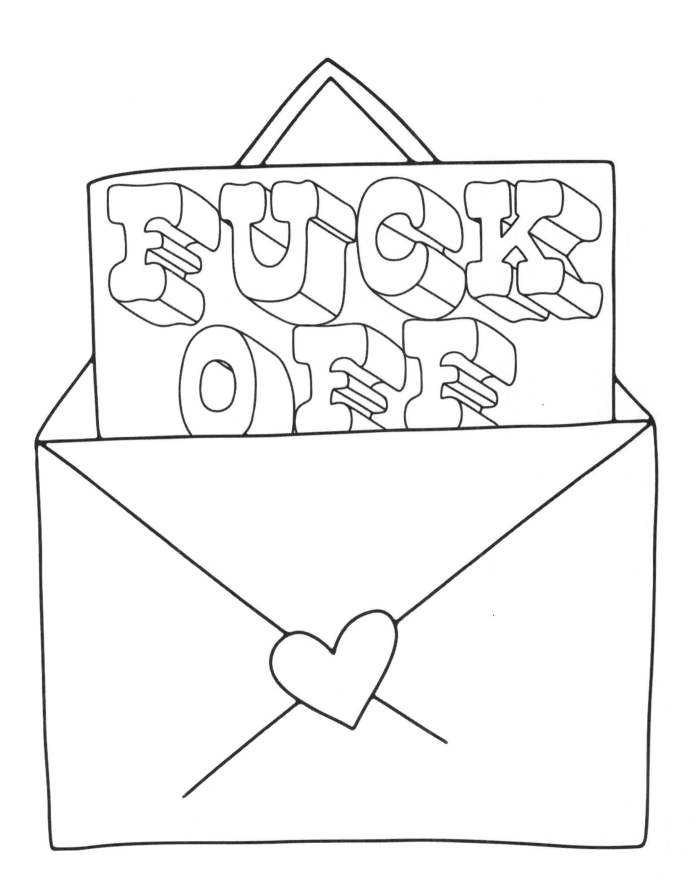

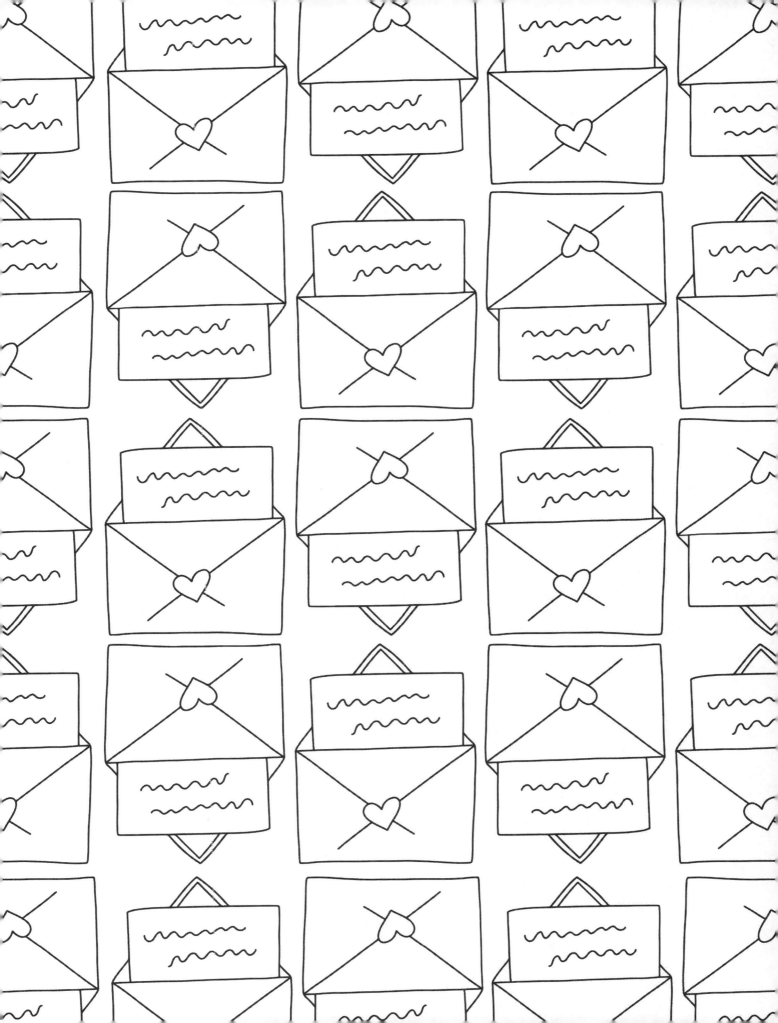

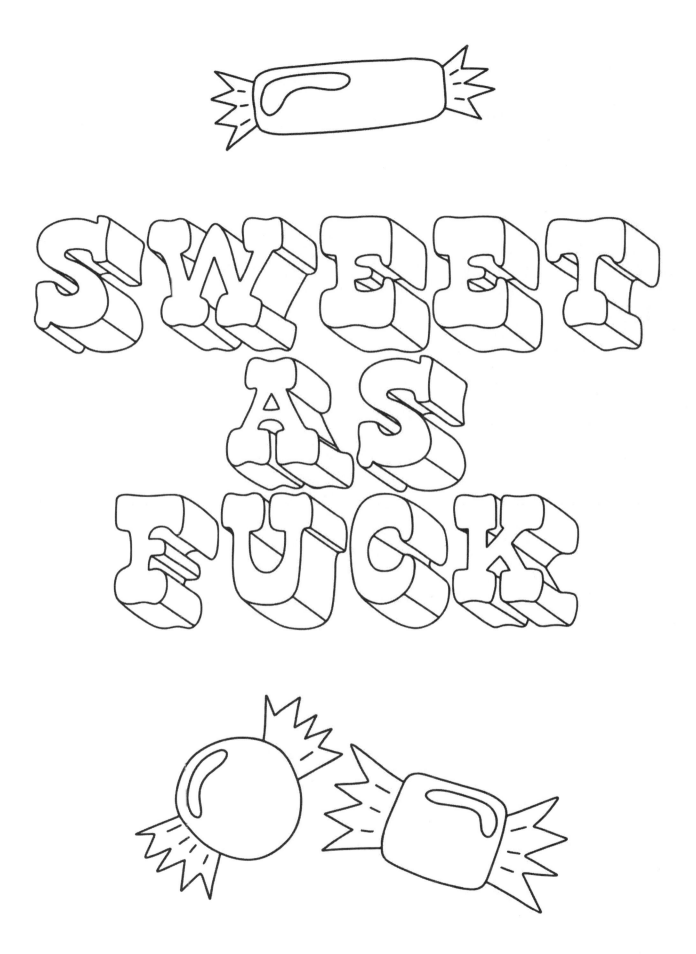

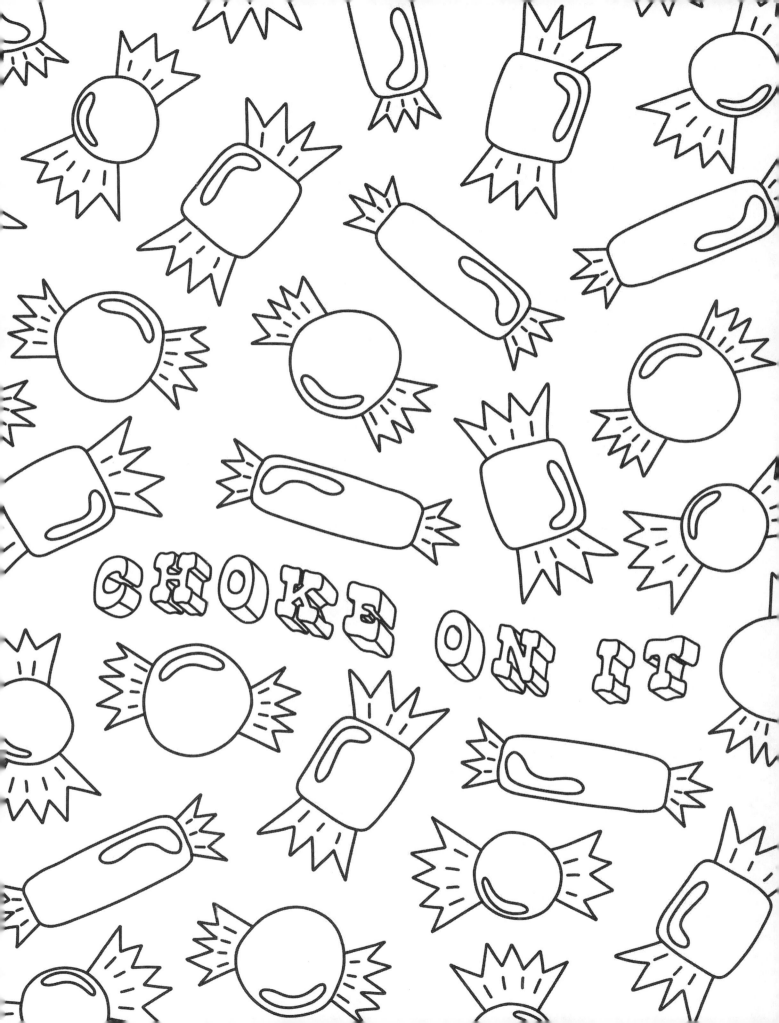

SAIL ALL THE WAY

THE FUCK AWAY FROM ME

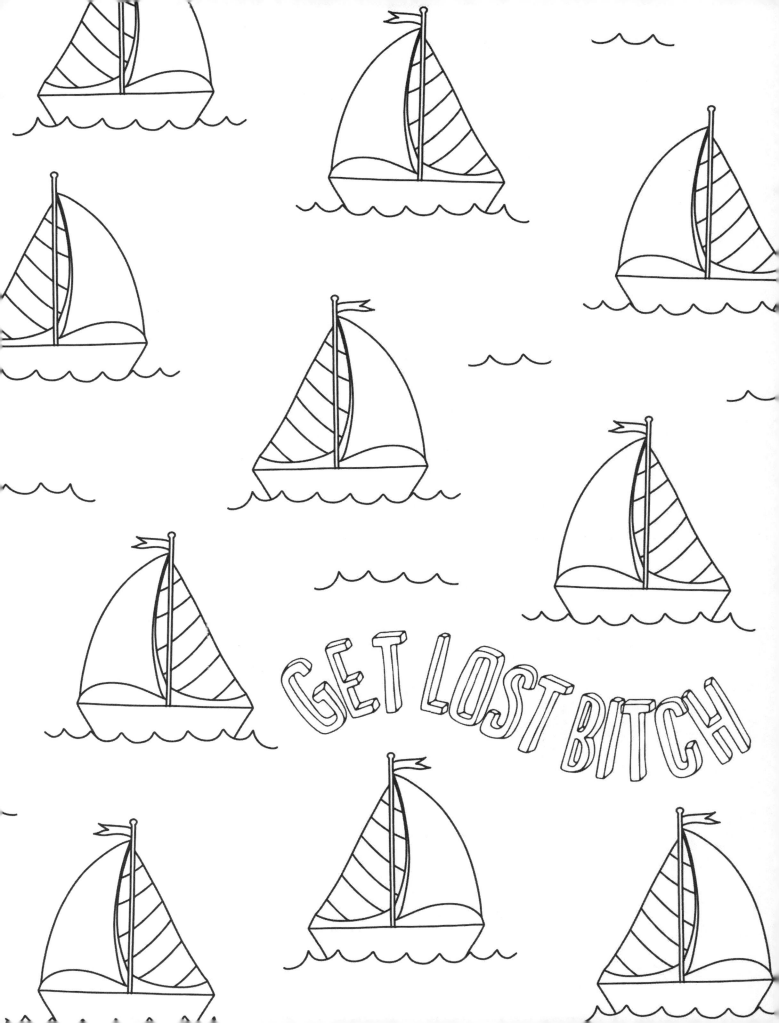

FUCK AROUND AND FIND OUT

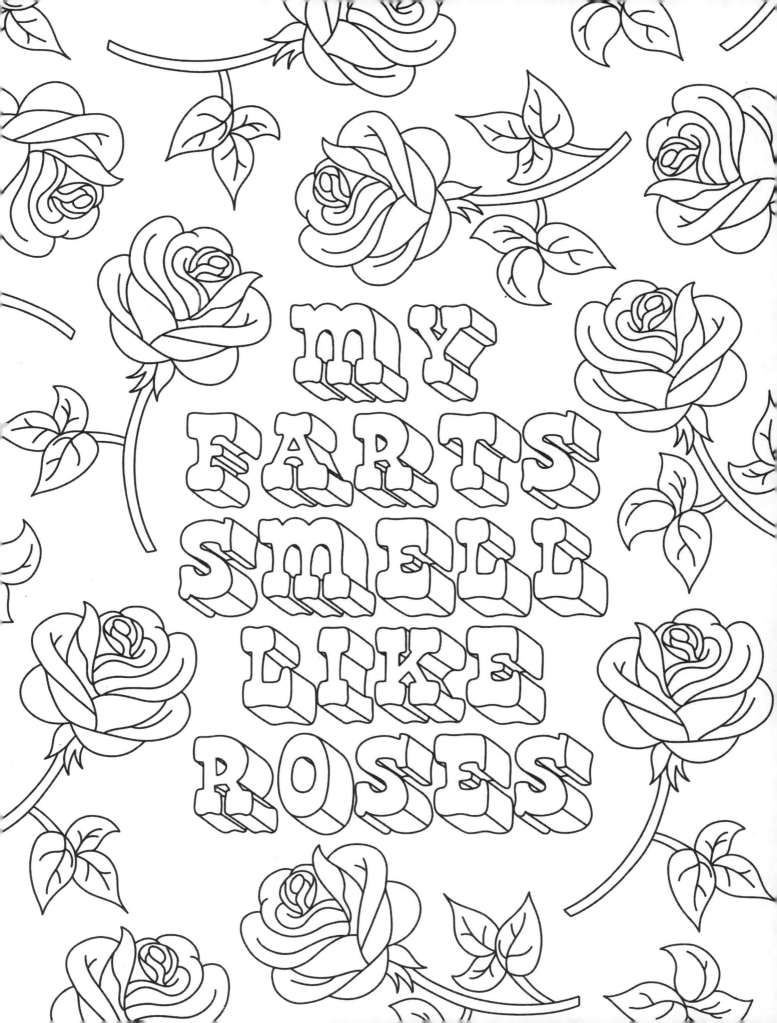

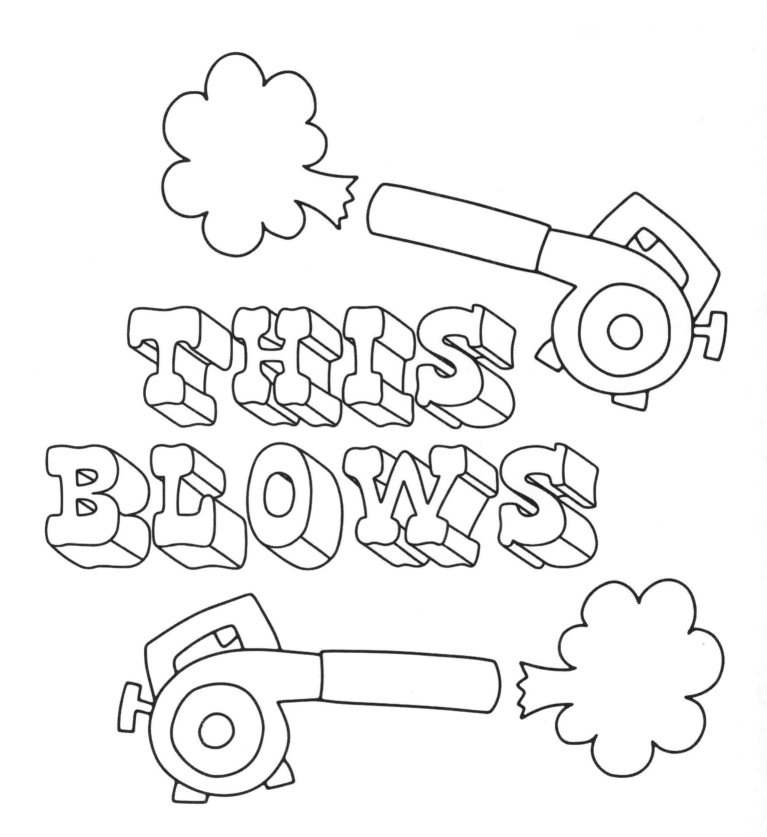

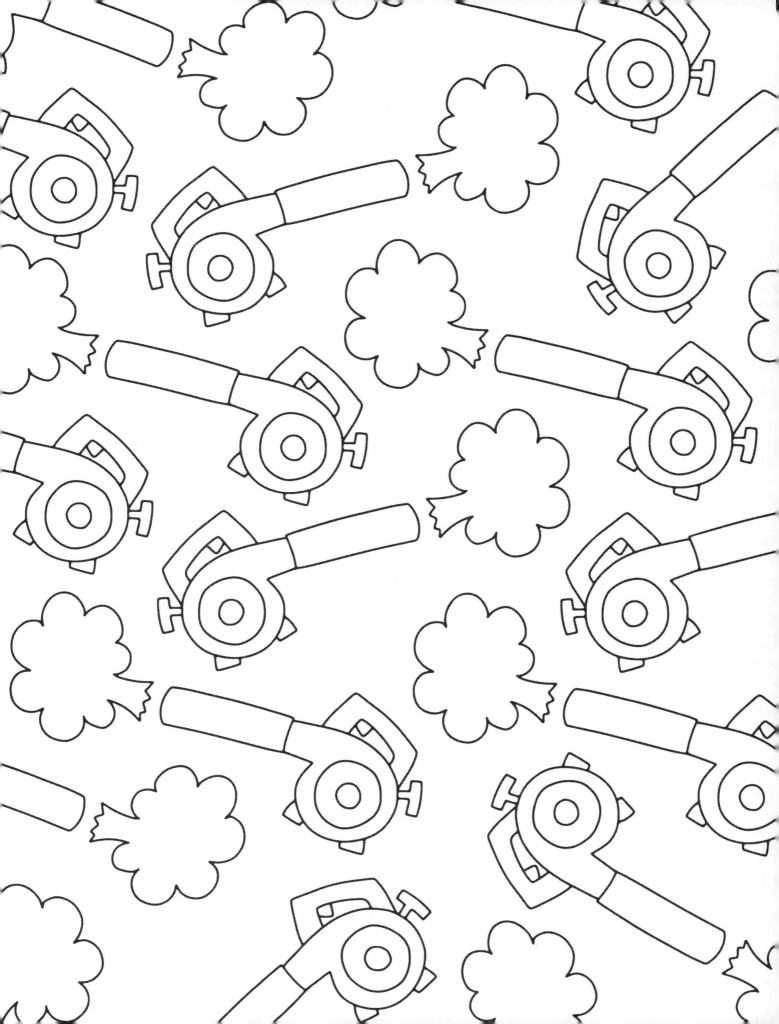

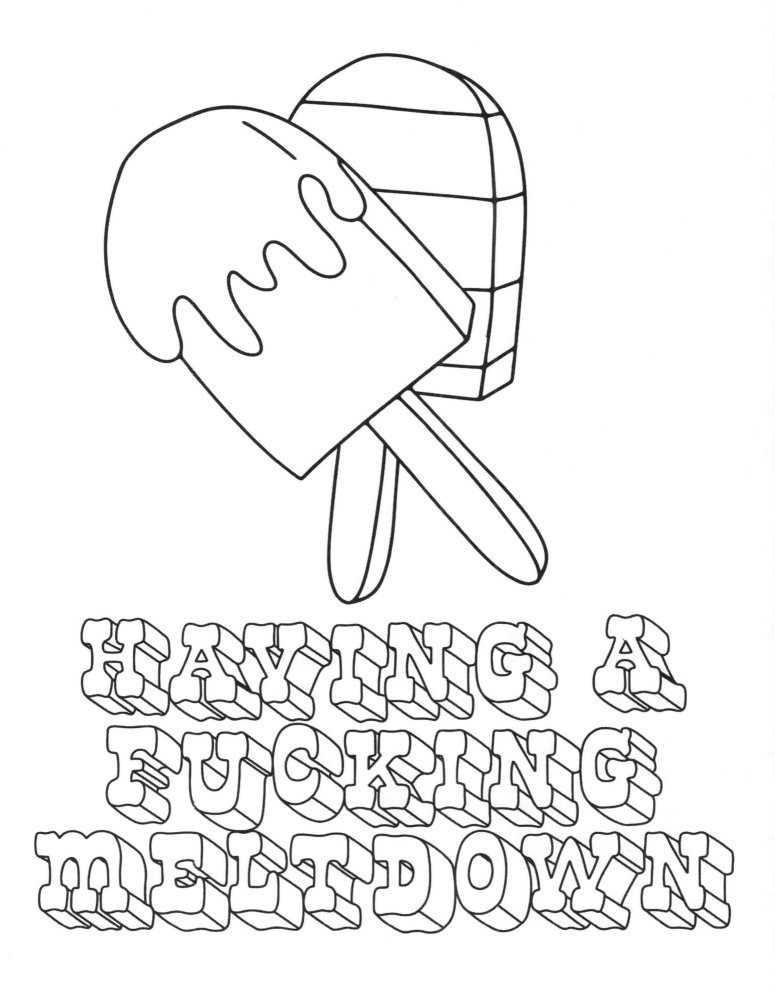

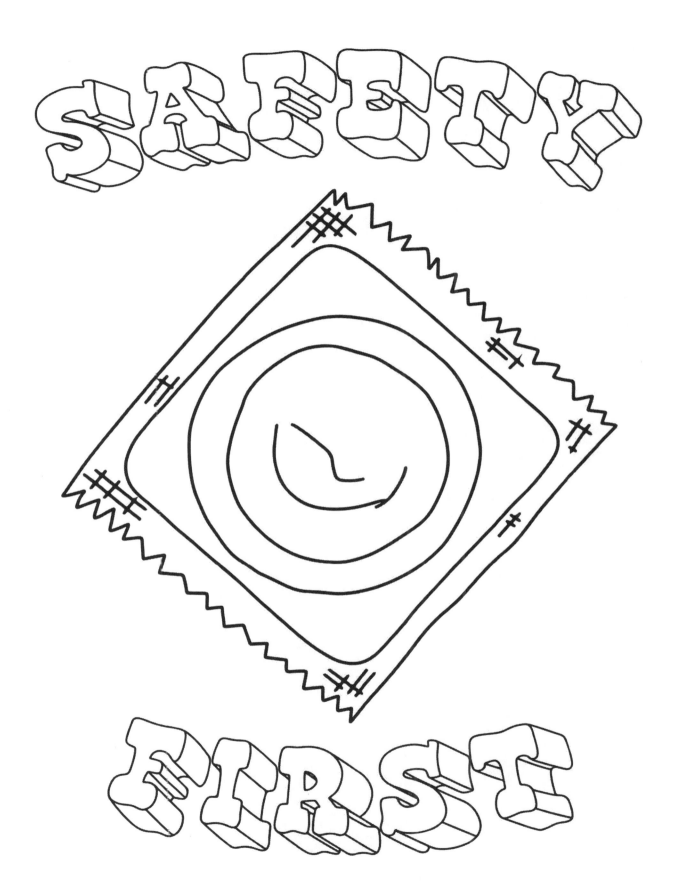

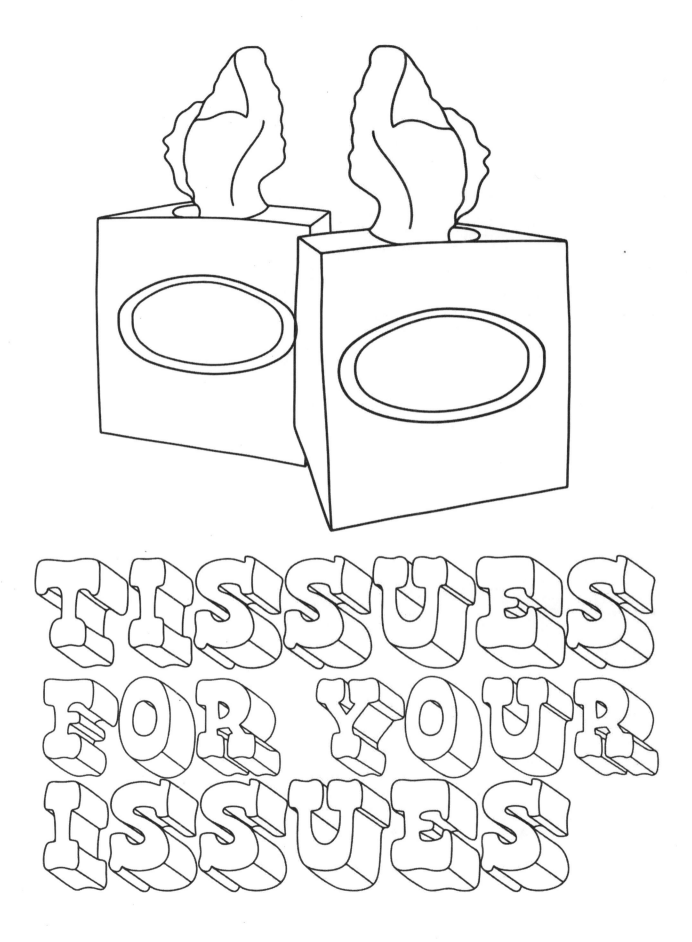

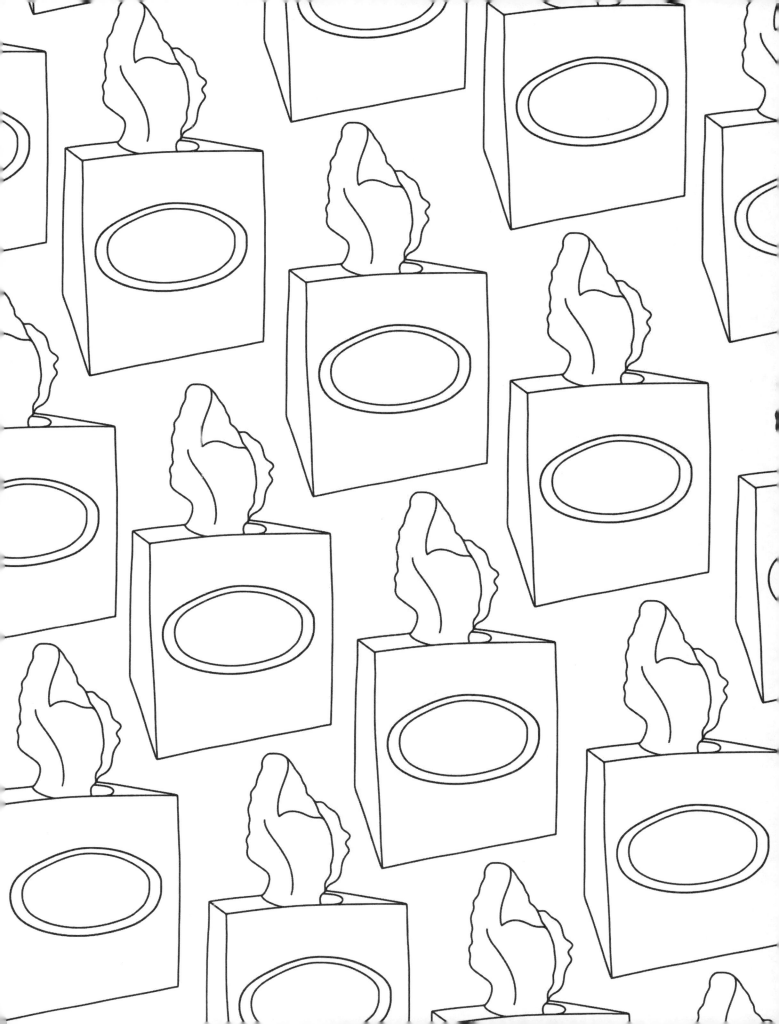

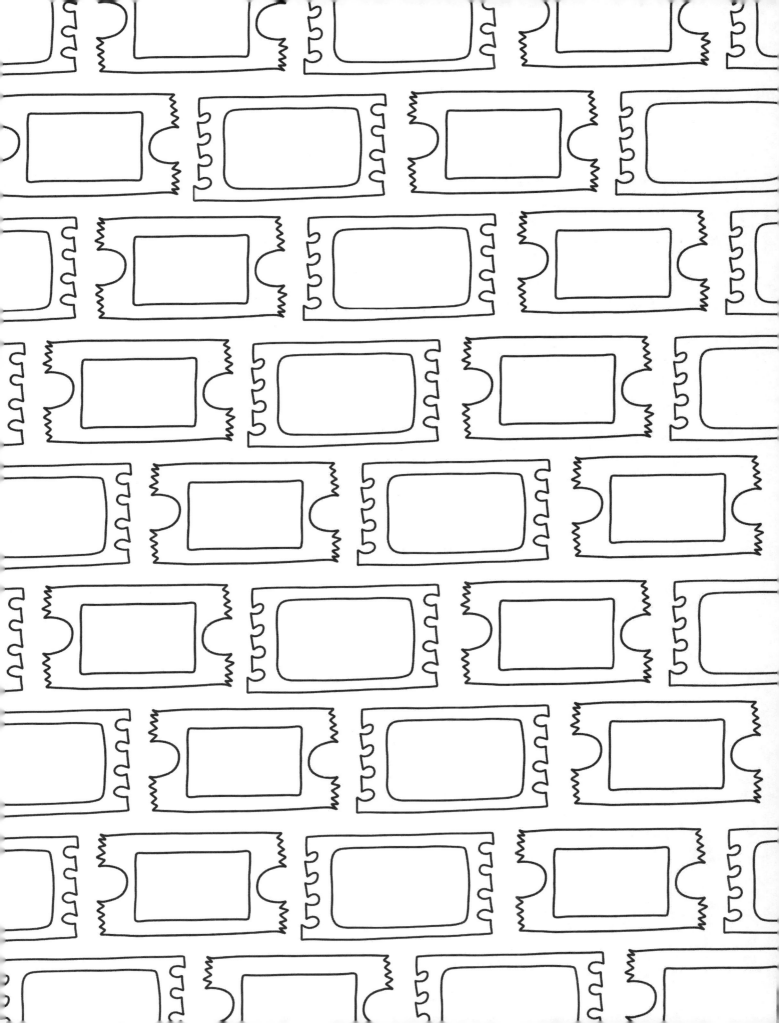

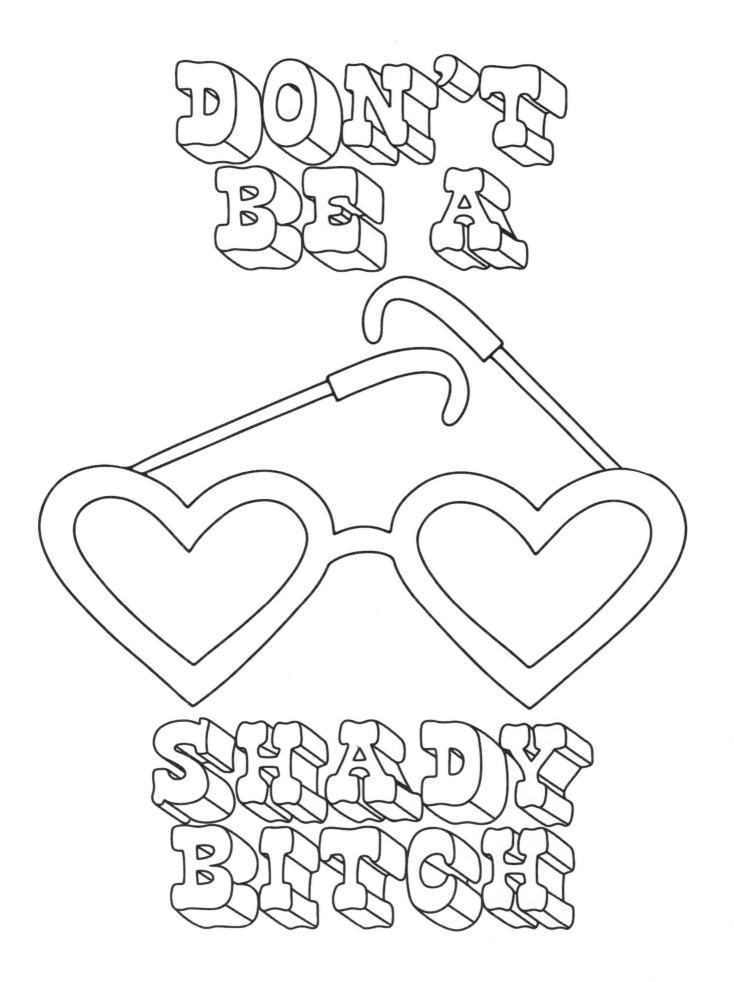

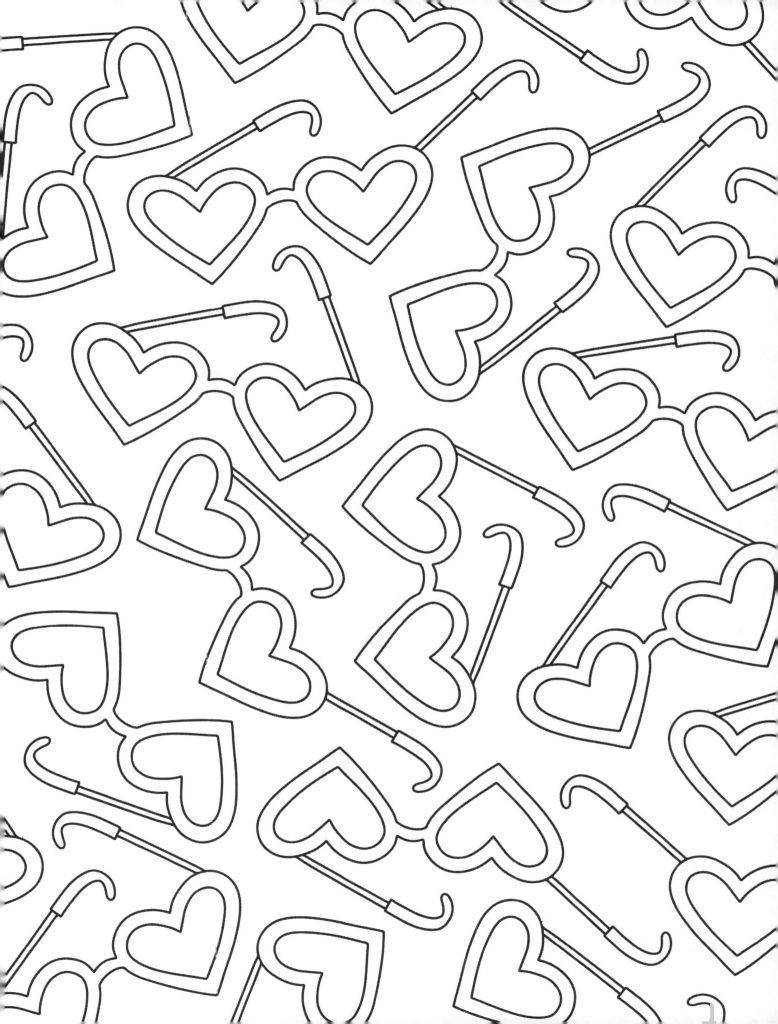

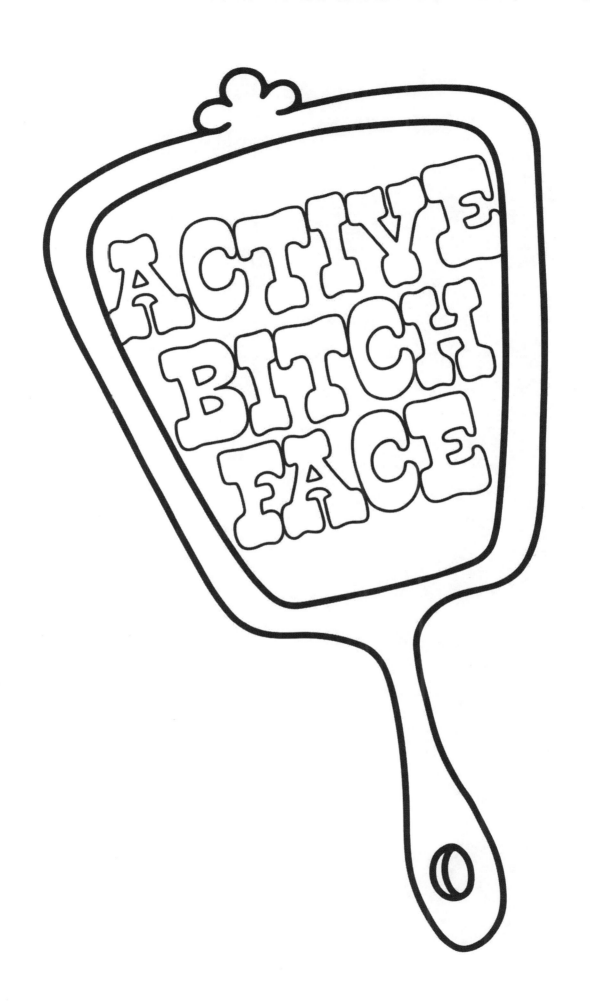

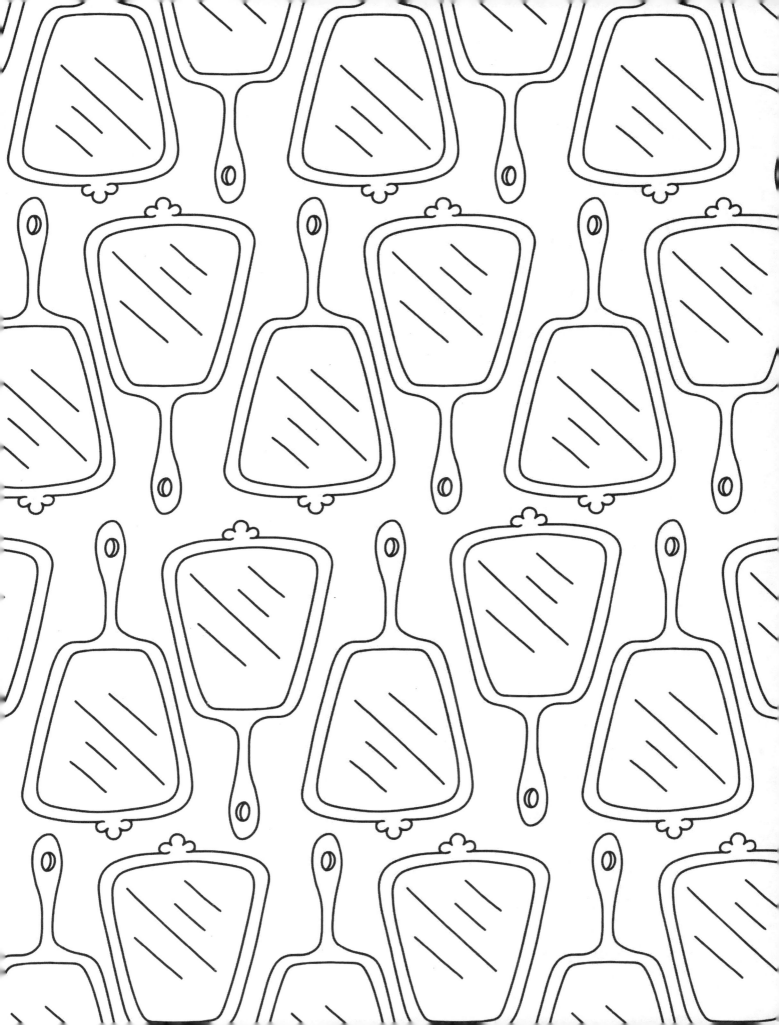

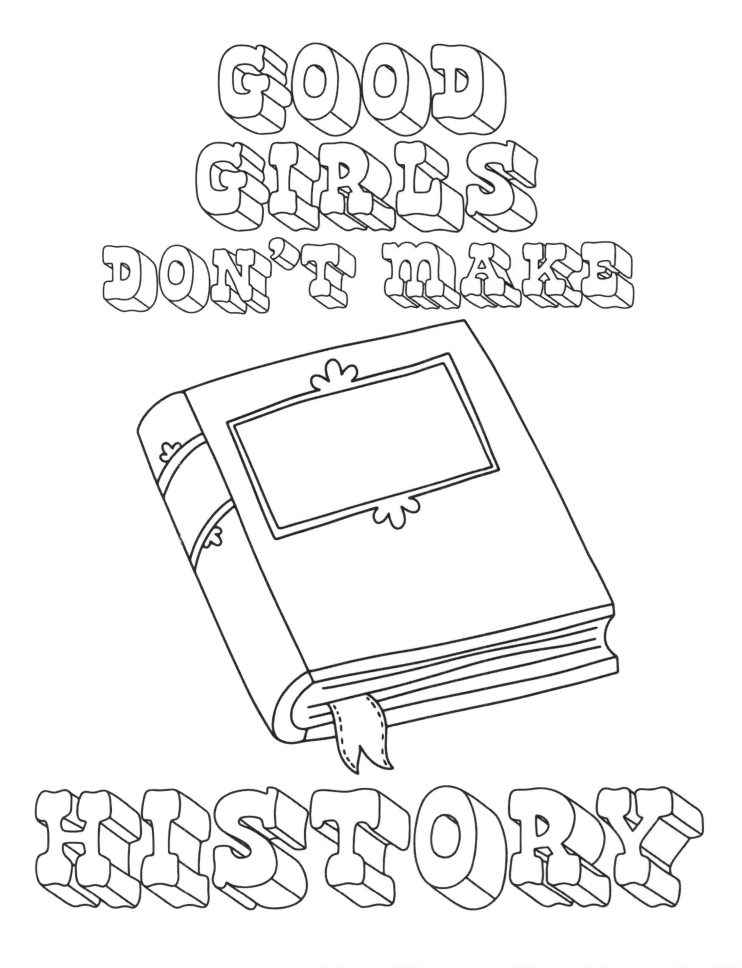

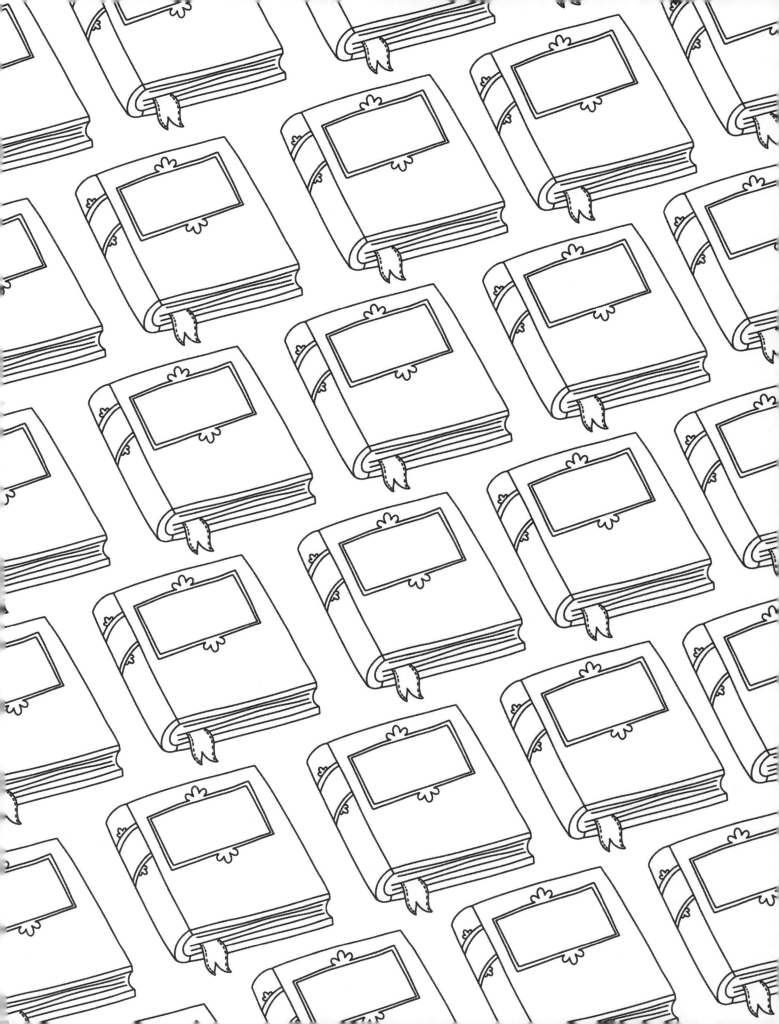

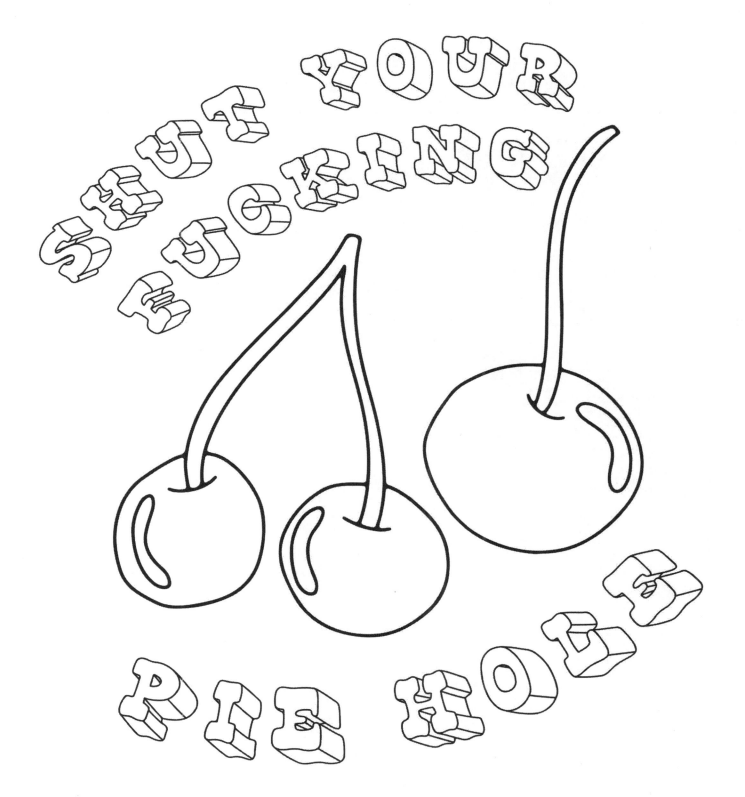

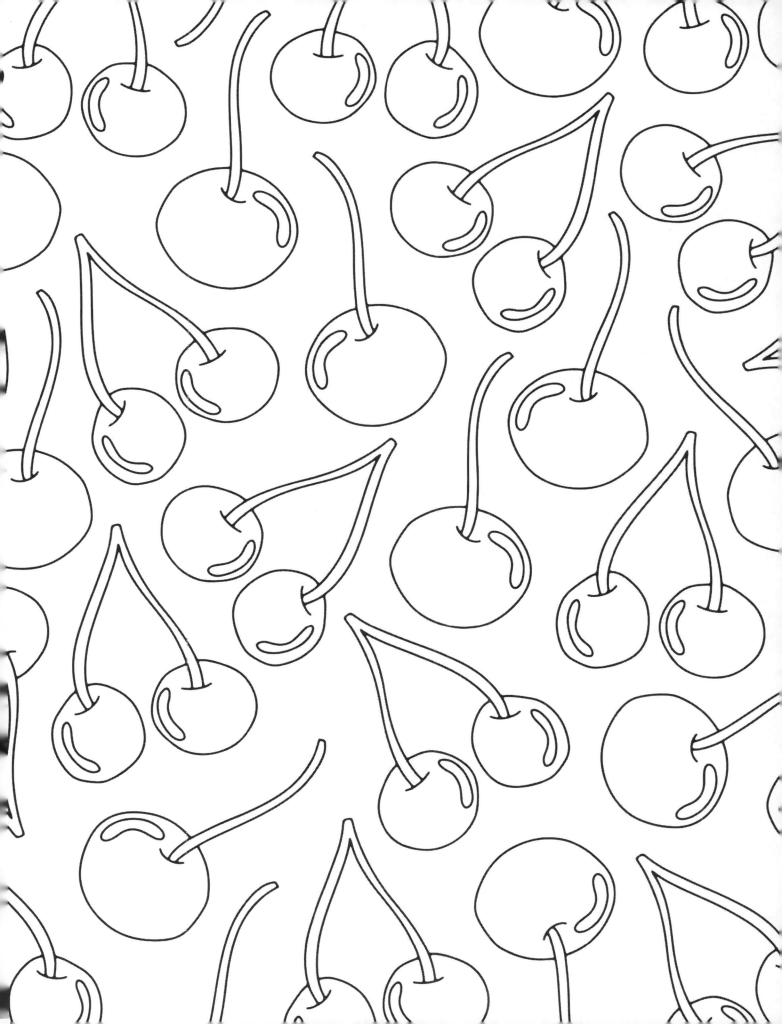

Made in the USA
Columbia, SC
03 September 2024

41406662R00043